Original title:
Where the Light Lives

Copyright © 2025 Creative Arts Management OÜ
All rights reserved.

Author: Jameson Hartfield
ISBN HARDBACK: 978-1-80581-884-7
ISBN PAPERBACK: 978-1-80581-411-5
ISBN EBOOK: 978-1-80581-884-7

Infinite Twinkles

Stars in the sky, winking bright,
Like fireflies dancing at night.
Why do they twinkle, you ask so bold?
They're just telling secrets, if truth be told.

A comet stumbles, a meteor slips,
They gather for gossip, with popcorn and chips.
They giggle and shine, like kids at play,
Turning the dark of night into bright ballet.

The Warmth of Knowing

In jackets so cozy, we gather 'round,
With laughter that echoes, a jovial sound.
A cup of hot cocoa, with marshmallows sweet,
Who knew being cozy could feel like a treat?

We tell silly stories, with humor so spry,
Like penguins ice-skating, oh my, oh my!
The warmth of our friendship, a glow that won't fade,
In this giggling circle, we've all got it made.

Touch of Gold

Sunshine peeks out, like a sneaky cat,
Painting the world in a hue, just like that.
A splash of bright laughter, a sprinkle of cheer,
More valuable than treasure, my dear, my dear!

In fields of dandelions, we tumble and roll,
Each flower a wish, each laugh a goal.
With friends at my side, I feel so bold,
For in every giggle, there's a touch of gold.

Echoes from the Light

The moon whispers jokes to the giggling trees,
While shadows do the cha-cha, as light hugs the leaves.
Oh, the crickets join in with a chirpy refrain,
Turning darkness to laughter, again and again!

Stars gather 'round in a cosmic dance,
Joking about planets, giving them a chance.
Echoes from the light, a playful parade,
Reminding us all, no worries are made.

The Sanctuary of Warmth

In a cozy chair, I sit and pry,
My cat's a detective, the world's awry.
Socks on my hands, the cold can't bite,
She judges my style, says I'm not quite right.

Cocoa spills like a mischievous elf,
I laugh at the thought; I can't help myself.
The heater hums a comforting tune,
While I plot my escape—maybe next June.

Reflections Under Starlit Skies

The stars above throw a glittery dance,
But my neighbor's dog thinks he's got a chance.
Barking in rhythm, with fervor so bold,
He thinks it's a concert, I'm just sold on cold.

I'd join their act, but I can't sing,
Maybe a tambourine would be my thing.
With moonlight chuckles, we share the night,
As dogs and I dream under twinkling light.

A Haven of Glorious Sparks

Fireflies flicker in a jester's parade,
While I hold a snack, oh, I'm so mislaid.
Chasing them down, but they take to the skies,
I trip over my feet while my grandma just sighs.

S'mores are a venture, a gooey delight,
But chocolate's now stuck on my nose—what a sight!
Giggles erupt with each melted bite,
In this silly haven, everything feels right.

The Heartbeat of Brightness

Bouncing around in socks full of fluff,
I test out the floors; oh, it's quite tough.
My dance is a sight, a fetch and a throw,
The dog's waltzing with me, releasing the glow.

The clock's striking chaos; it's time for a snack,
And I plan my grand heist to sneak in the bag.
There's laughter in harvest, there's joy in the mess,
In this heartbeat of fun, oh, I must confess!

Whispers of the Sun

In a world so dim, the sun did shout,
'Take a break, my friend, don't pout!'
With laughter bright, it danced on down,
Making shadows wear a frown.

It tickled leaves and sparked the air,
Brought giggles to the old oak's hair.
As flowers spun in dizzy glee,
They whispered secrets, wild and free.

A sneaky beam peered through the trees,
Winking at the dancing bees.
Each ray a joke, a playful tease,
Bringing grins like sweet sunny breeze.

So if you feel the world is gray,
Just listen close; hear what they say.
The sun is here with jokes galore,
Spreading cheer forevermore!

A Glimmer in the Gloom

Amidst the clouds, a sparkle sparked,
A little glow, it cheerily remarked,
"Don't be sad, just look up high,
I'm the twinkle in your eye!"

The shadow friends all rolled their eyes,
"Oh goodness, look who's trying to rise!"
But the glimmer wouldn't frown or hide,
It'd tickle raindrops, let hope glide.

A firefly faintly joined the glow,
Said, "Together, let's steal the show!"
So they bounced from gloom to prankish cheer,
Leaving laughter for all to hear.

So when the days feel far too drear,
Remember that flicker, hold it dear.
A sparkle's all it takes to bloom,
In life's jolly little room.

Sanctuary of Brightness

In a cozy nook, a beam took rest,
Declared, "This spot is simply the best!"
With laughter echoing through the air,
It gathered friends, a lively fair.

A chubby cloud with a cheeky grin,
Joined the fun with a playful spin.
"You can't outshine me!" it joked with flair,
As sunlight tickled the fluffy hair.

With giggles glowing, and shadows mild,
Even grumpies were quickly reviled.
In this haven, joy did abide,
With each smile counted, a radiant ride.

So if you feel a shadow loom,
Head to the spot where giggles bloom.
For in this warmth, you'll find relief,
And share in the fun, beyond belief.

The Radiance Within

Deep in the heart, a spark did dwell,
Waiting patiently to ring the bell.
It whispered softly, a jester's tune,
"Let's not wait for the sun at noon!"

With a twinkle here, and a chuckle there,
It painted grins from ear to ear.
Like a cheeky sprite in a playful race,
Lighting up even the gloomiest place.

As moments passed, it grew so bright,
It wrapped the world in pure delight.
"Why wait for dusk? Let's glow all day!"
And danced on laughter, come what may.

So dig deep, find your inner sun,
It's always there, ready for fun.
For in each of us, a giggle shines,
Creating joy that soars and climbs.

Dreams Entwined in Light

In the garden of giggles, we play,
Where the sun spills laughter like confetti all day.
Chasing shadows with jolly old jesters,
Tickling clouds, we're the merry investors.

With a wink from the moon, we dance on our toes,
A parade of odd socks, nobody knows.
We juggle with rainbows, a whimsical sight,
And drink lemonade made of pure, fizzy light.

Canvas of Radiance

On a canvas of pancakes, we flip with delight,
Painting syrup suns, oh what a sweet sight!
We sprinkle some giggles, a dash of not-bored,
As creatures of whimsy emerge and adored.

With crayons of sunshine, we color the bees,
Chasing the shadows with glittery keys.
As laughter drips honey from trees made of cheer,
We dance through a landscape of joy, oh so clear.

Beyond the Horizon's Gleam

With binoculars made of licorice twirls,
We spy on the silliness that brightly unfurls.
Beyond the horizon, where sneakers take flight,
The land of the chuckles glows funny and bright.

A boat made of chocolates, we sail with a sound,
While marshmallow whales jump, fun's all around.
The clouds wear pajamas; the stars sing a tune,
As moonbeams play hopscotch beneath the big moon.

A Journey to Warmth

On a train of hot cocoa, we chug down the lane,
With marshmallow cabin crew, delightful, no bane.
Through hills of soft giggles, we travel with glee,
As funny little rabbits play banjos, oh me!

We'll stop at the station called Sillyville square,
Where everyone's laughing without a big care.
With each burst of humor, the warmth starts to rise,
In a world filled with giggles beneath smiling skies.

Tapestry of Shining Moments

In a world of mismatched socks,
Laughter dances with the clocks.
Jelly beans and silly hats,
We chase our dreams like flying rats.

Noses pressed on frost-kissed glass,
Every mishap tops the class.
Spilled juice colors every laugh,
Finding joy in life's rough draft.

Balloons afloat beyond our reach,
Squirrels teach us how to breach.
Why do we trip on our own feet?
Because falling's just a rhythm beat.

Tickling tales around the fire,
Chasing sparks that don't expire.
In this tapestry we weave,
Each stitch a joy, we won't believe!

Flickers of Forgotten Joy

Whispers of a prank gone wrong,
Dancing like a silly song.
Forgotten toys and missing shoes,
Chasing down those childhood views.

In a pile of laundry, peek-a-boo,
Yarn tangled in a playful coup.
Giggles echo through the breeze,
While the cat twirls with utmost ease.

Ice cream drips and runs away,
Melting fast, but hey, let's play!
Finding treasure in the trash,
Building dreams with every splash.

Rusty bikes and wobbly rides,
Sunshine waits where laughter hides.
In these flickers, we renew,
The joyful spark we once all knew.

A Journey Through Radiant Memories

With a map drawn on a napkin,
Adventure's waiting, can you tap in?
Lost in a forest of old toys,
We stumble upon our forgotten joys.

Zany hats and mismatched shoes,
Unicorns dance, no time to snooze.
Tickling cousins, as we sprint,
Their laughter, a melodious hint.

Silly selfies with goofy grins,
Ten-point-five on the scale of sins.
Each snapshot captures the best,
As our memories put us to the test.

Chocolate-covered everything,
Laughter makes our hearts take wing.
As we journey with smiles bold,
Each radiant tale is a treasure worth gold.

Grace in Glowing Shadows

In every shadow, a giggle hides,
Moonbeams drip like silly slides.
Dancing with shadows, laughter rings,
Comedic grace is what life brings.

Mismatched dreams on the floor lay,
Like a puzzling game we play.
Wiggling toes in clumsy dance,
Finding joy in every chance.

Chasing light with bubble gum,
Sticky fingers, not so dumb.
Cartwheeling through the starry night,
What a sight, our silly flight!

In the glow, we find our spark,
Twisting tales till it's past dark.
Graceful laughs and silly songs,
In these shadows, nothing's wrong.

Threads of Radiance

In a world of tangled socks,
The sun plays peek-a-boo with clocks.
Laughter weaves through every seam,
Chasing shadows like a dream.

When the cat jumps and bumps the light,
It's a disco party, oh what a sight!
Reflecting beams on the wall so grand,
Turning the room into a dance wonderland.

Silly ducks waddling in a row,
They quack in rhythm, putting on a show.
Sunbeams tickle their feathered toes,
As they strut their stuff in evening glows.

A cup of joy spills on the floor,
The coffee dances, what's in store?
With giggles shared and brightness spread,
Life's a party, let's go ahead!

A Symphony of Glows

The moon plays violin to stars so bright,
While crickets tap dance with all their might.
A comedy of sounds fills the night,
Casting giggles in the pale moonlight.

Jellybeans bounce on the table's edge,
Their sugary laughs are like a pledge.
A chorus of sweets in the evening air,
Where every note is a candy affair.

Frogs in chorus sing a round,
With splashes of joy that abound.
Fireflies join in, twinkling away,
Making the shadows twirl and sway.

Together we weave this bright serenade,
With laughter and light that never fades.
Silly symphonies in a cosmic show,
Turning the mundane into a glow!

Guiding Stars

Twinkling laughter lights the skies,
As stars play hide and seek with our eyes.
Comets zoom with their flashy tails,
Chasing giggles through glittery trails.

Aliens hula-hoop in the night,
Their fluorescent dance is quite the sight.
Wobbling like jellies in the breeze,
Stealing wishes from jellybean trees.

The moon sips tea with the wise old owl,
Who tells silly tales with a thoughtful scowl.
Shooting stars crash with a friendly cheer,
Each burst of light brings us all near.

So grab a spark from the starlit spree,
And let your heart dance wild and free.
With every twinkle, a chuckle shared,
In the laughter-filled night, no one is scared!

Beneath the Aureate Canopy

Under the sun's disco ball sway,
Dancing daisies come out to play.
With petals swishing in the breeze,
They throw fun parties, if you please.

The sunflowers wear sunglasses bright,
Striking poses in golden light.
With goofy grins and stems that twirl,
They invite you for a giggling whirl.

Bees buzz like tiny planes in flight,
Tickling trees, filled with delight.
In this garden of chuckles and blooms,
Every corner bursts with joy that looms.

So when life gets heavy and clouds appear,
Look for the silly; it's always near.
For under this golden, glowing dome,
Laughter and warmth always feel like home!

The Lanterns of Tomorrow

In the drawer of old socks,
I found lanterns made of cheese,
They giggled and glowed so bright,
Chasing my worries with ease.

They dance on my windowsill,
In a conga line so swell,
Telling jokes to the shadows,
Lighting up my little cell.

With beams of laughter and fun,
They spark joy from dusk till dawn,
I swear they're powered by giggles,
And toast from the bread that's gone!

So here's to the future's glow,
With fireworks made of smiles,
Let's twirl in the brilliant haze,
And enjoy these silly trials!

Places of Glowing Hope

In a place where dreams are hats,
And muffins sing the blues,
Hope is served on a silver plate,
With sprinkles of silly clues.

The alley cats wear sneakers,
While owls hoot out a beat,
They throw a disco party,
Making twilight feel so sweet.

Each corner has a secret,
A tickle, a wink, a grin,
Glimmers chase away the frowns,
And every place feels like kin.

So grab a slice of fairy pie,
Join the fun in this dear space,
Let laughter light the way for us,
In this warm and cozy place!

Whispers in the Golden Glow

When the toaster starts to hum,
And the kettle winks at me,
Whispers float through crisp morning air,
Like sugar-spiced jubilee.

Socks that dance on the floor,
Chairs that giggle out loud,
They share their secrets with the sun,
And wrap me in a shroud.

The curtain winks conspiratorially,
As daylight rocks its tune,
I trip on my own two feet,
And laugh with the golden moon.

Oh, where do all these whispers go?
To a party, I believe,
In a world of warm delight,
Where even the lamps can grieve!

The Hearth of Daydreams

In the hearth of my mind's delight,
Daydreams gather around the flame,
They roast marshmallows of silly thoughts,
And play a very quirky game.

A unicorn juggles stars,
While squirrels wear tiny hats,
They sip on rainbow punch,
And invite all the fancy cats.

Giggles crackle in the air,
As visions prance and slide,
With joy spilling over the edges,
And imagination as our guide.

So let's stoke the fire bright,
And fan the silly dreams,
For in this hearth of wonder,
Life bursts at the seams!

Beneath the Golden Canopy

In the park where shadows play,
Squirrels dance, hip-hop all day.
Sunbeams tickle, leaves all sway,
Chasing giggles, bright and gay.

Picnic ants have crazy dreams,
Building towers, or so it seems.
Winking sun with golden beams,
Makes us laugh till our sides scream.

Beneath this bright and sunny dome,
We discover joy, our playful home.
With each snort, each little groan,
Nature's stage, where humor's grown.

So grab a snack, and let's all run,
In this circus, life's just fun.
Under the sky, joy's never done,
Beneath the gold, we laugh and pun.

Embrace the Shine

In a world where gleams collide,
Hats with feathers, and birds that ride.
Fuzzy socks on sunshine's side,
We flip and flail, with hearts so wide.

Neighbors twirl in shades so bright,
Dancing llamas, what a sight!
Handstands with a twist of light,
As we tumble, oh what a flight!

Laughter echoes, bounces round,
Funny faces, silly sounds.
With each giggle, joy is found,
Where the warmth and fun abound.

The sun's embrace, a silly tease,
As we waddle with such ease.
A joyful crew, like buzzing bees,
Chasing rays, we're sure to please.

Dawn's Soft Embrace

As dawn peeks with a blushing grin,
Cats in PJs, let the day begin!
Coffee spills, oh where to bin?
Chasing dreams, let the laughter spin.

Sunshine yawns, stretches its rays,
That cozy blanket, it now sways.
Breakfast dances in absurd plays,
Burnt toast sings about 'better days'.

The morning crew, we're quite the clan,
Making shadows, oh what a plan!
With each giggle, we form a band,
Under the sun, let's take a stand.

So let's embrace this wacky morn,
With sticky fingers, we are reborn.
A symphony of joy is sworn,
In dawn's embrace, love's never worn.

Threads of Illumination

Stitching smiles with every thread,
Laughter bursts, no need for lead.
Under umbrellas, where fun is spread,
Pulling jokes from the sky, well-fed.

Knitting clouds with whimsical grace,
We poke fun at the sun's bright face.
Each snicker weaves a warm embrace,
In this fabric of joy, we find our place.

Socks that spark, and hats so strange,
With every twist, our thoughts exchange.
We wear our quirks like a badge of range,
In threads of light, we boldly change.

So raise your needle, let's create,
A tapestry that celebrates fate.
With each new stitch, we elevate,
In this glow, we levitate.

The Light's Gentle Hand

In a world of shadows that dance and prance,
A glow walks in with a chuckling glance.
It tickles the flowers, it wiggles the trees,
And whispers to everyone, "Just laugh, if you please!"

With a wink of the sun, it plays tag at noon,
Twirling the clouds to a silly tune.
The bees buzz in rhythm, all buzzing around,
As the light streams in, making giggles abound.

It splashes on puddles, makes rainbows bob,
Turns a grumpy cat into a cheerful blob.
When shadows start stretching, light chuckles and glows,
Saying, "Don't worry, I'm here, full of bows!"

So if you feel down, just look for this friend,
Who dances in colors that never quite end.
With a flick and a flash, life's not quite a bore,
As the light's gentle hand shows you humor galore.

Waves of Radiance

The sun rides the waves like a surfboard pro,
Splashing bright giggles from to and fro.
The ocean reflects, with a wink and a grin,
As light ricochets from fins of a fishy kin.

Watch the seagulls soar with a comic flair,
They squawk silly songs, like they just don't care.
Sunbeams are surfboards, dancing on blue,
Riding through laughter, fresh as morning dew.

A crab in a tuxedo, all dapper and neat,
Takes a bow to the tide, then admits defeat.
For the light waves in with a froggy cheer,
Saying, "Let's have a party; the beach is right here!"

So grab your shades, let's hit the sand,
The glow of the sun makes everything grand.
In waves of bright chuckles and sparkling cheers,
Life's a sunny joke that tickles our ears!

A Love Letter to Dusk

Dear Dusk, you're a sneak, as day turns to night,
With colors that twinkle, oh, what a sight!
You cuddle the stars, settle them in snug,
While whispering secrets with a mischievous shrug.

Oh, how you tease with your shimmery glow,
Turning clouds into candy, all pink and aglow.
You dance with the shadows, skipping along,
Making the crickets chirp a silly song.

You dress the night up in velvety charm,
And wrap the moon tight in your cozy balm.
Each flicker of twilight is a wink and a sigh,
As fireflies twirl, saying, "Me? Oh, my!"

So here's to you, Dusk, with your whimsical flare,
A love letter bright, for you, I declare.
In your golden embrace, we laugh and we sway,
For you're the cheeky end to our bright sunny day!

Luminescence Beneath the Surface

In a pond where frogs wear hats,
And fireflies do silly dances,
The goldfish share their gossip too,
About the duck's latest prances.

The sun makes all the colors pop,
While turtles wear their shades with flair,
They strike a pose on lily pads,
And wink at all who stop and stare.

Beneath the waves, a party's on,
The squids have got some ink to spill,
They're drawing doodles on the sand,
And giving themselves quite the thrill.

So dive, let's see what fun we find,
With laughter bubbling all about,
In this bright world where whimsy thrives,
Join in! There's joy without a doubt.

The Sanctuary of Radiant Dreams

In a land where pillows sing at night,
And teddy bears hold court with glee,
The moon hangs low, like a sleepy cat,
While stars trade jokes at the marquee.

Upside down in daydreams' keep,
The rabbits wear tuxedos neat,
They throw a tea party with pies galore,
As cupcakes fidget on tiny feet.

Cotton candy clouds float nearby,
Sprinkling sugar with every gust,
While unicorns roll their eyes at jokes,
And giggle, for it's a must!

So wander here, where the silly thrives,
In a sanctuary of kooky schemes,
Where laughter mingles with the breeze,
In every corner of our dreams.

Illuminated Horizons

On a beach where seagulls wear a tie,
And surfboards converse with a cheer,
The waves are dressed in sparkly coats,
As crabs moonwalk, with nothing to fear.

Kites fly high, doing silly flips,
While the sun beams down in a cozy blaze,
And flip-flops dance along the shore,
In their best impression of the craze.

Sandcastles groan under the weight,
Of buckets filled with dreams and schemes,
Mermaids giggle just out of sight,
While snorkelers plot their funny themes.

The horizon glows with colors bright,
As daytime waves a cheerful goodbye,
And the breezy tunes keep spirits high,
Under the vast, unending sky.

Beyond the Shadows

In a park where shadows play hide and seek,
Squirrels wear masks made from leaves,
They squabble 'bout nuts in a playful way,
While giggling at the stories that weave.

The sun dons a hat, as funny as can be,
And tickles the flowers to make them grin,
The daisies sway, sharing silly tales,
Of what happens when the day begins.

Beneath the bench, a rabbit's in charge,
Holding court with a group of ants,
They plot a parade of marshmallow treats,
While crickets scratch out quirky chants.

So if you wander down this path,
Where laughter dances in brilliant hues,
You'll find the joy beyond the dark,
Where shadows find their rhythm and muse.

A Song of Radiance

In a room full of shadows, I dance with delight,
Making the dark laugh at my silly sight.
With a cap on my head, all colors so bright,
Even the gloom can't resist the invite!

I twirl and I spin, like a dervish in glee,
My socks mismatched, oh what a sight to see!
I shine with ridiculous charm, can't you see?
Bringing chuckles to all, like a ticklish bee.

Bright bulbs above me, they flicker in fun,
Whispering secrets, sharing a pun.
Together we giggle 'til the day is all done,
Twirling in sunlight, all worries we shun.

So join in the frolic, don't hide from the cheer,
Laughter makes everything feel far more clear.
Let's brighten the world, spread joy far and near,
With radiant moments that we hold so dear.

The Light of Being

Wake up with a chuckle, a grin on your face,
Sunshine spilling laughter all over the place.
Good vibes in the morning, it's a holiday race,
A tickle of warmth that you can't help but chase.

Traffic light dances, a samba in red,
Cars honk like they're singing, it's all in your head!
Sidewalks are giggling, no need to tread,
Just hop with your heart, let joy be your thread.

The birds crack jokes as they soar in the sky,
They pause for a moment, wink with a sigh.
Each feather a quip, each landing a hi,
Laughter soothes like a warm cupcake pie.

So bask in the nonsense, dance like a fool,
In the glow of the absurd, we create our own rule.
Every snicker a treasure, each snort a jewel,
In this bright-hearted life, humor's the fuel.

Brilliant Threads

In a quilt made of giggles, I wrap up at night,
Patchwork of laughter, oh what a delight!
Each square a story, each stitch we ignite,
Chasing away darkness, oh what a fight!

A ceiling of stars, they're throwing a bash,
Twinkling like fireflies, covering in flash.
They tease with their winks, like kids with a splash,
Each glow a reminder, life's never too brash.

The moon makes a face, all silly and bright,
Rolling her eyes at the joke of the night.
Clouds join the fun, in their fluffy white flight,
Spreading laughter like confetti, all stories unite.

So weave in the chuckles, let joy interlace,
In our brilliant tapestry, we'll always find space.
For laughter's a thread, that time can't erase,
In the fabric of moments, it sets the pace.

Flicker of Hope

In the corners of chaos, a giggle escapes,
A flicker of hope, in the silliest shapes.
The cat on the windowsill, dreaming of grapes,
Is plotting a heist, in a world full of scrapes.

Shadows whisper secrets, they join in the jest,
With a shimmy and shake, they put laughter to test.
They tickle the walls, with silly requests,
Saying, "Life's a big game, come give it your best!"

A puppy in socks, tries to prance with pride,
His wiggly tail tells where his joy will slide.
Dropping his toys, what a comical ride,
In a waltz with the wind, he takes it all in stride.

So raise a glass high, to the goofy and bright,
To the mishaps and giggles that banish the night.
In the flicker of moments, we find the pure light,
In laughter's embrace, we feel ever so right.

Candlelight Memories

In a room filled with flickering glee,
A cat's tail swishes like a candle's spree.
Grandma's tales, all giggles and grins,
As we dance with shadows, where the fun begins.

Bouncing shadows on the wall,
A knock at the door made us all fall.
With a whoopee cushion and a hearty cheer,
We celebrate moments that bring us near.

Mismatched socks and silly hats,
We laughed until we fell flat.
Candle wax drips like life's silly tricks,
In every flicker, a new giggle sticks.

So here's to nights with friends by the flame,
Where laughter blooms and none feel shame.
As candles burn low and memories rise,
There's humor in shadows, a joyful surprise.

Splendor in the Shadows

In corners where giggles softly tread,
Silhouettes prance, never misled.
Dancing in sunlight and moon's sweet smile,
We twirl in shadows, embracing the style.

Our shadows stretch, playing tricks on the floor,
Making faces and flops, we can't help but roar.
Like a comedy show without a script,
In the dark, our humor is wildly equipped.

A pair of socks that never match,
In the dim, they're a source of a fun patch.
Scrapbooks of laughter, coffee stains,
In low-light moments, our joy remains.

Through splendor and silliness, we unite,
In laughter's embrace, everything feels right.
So let's dance through shadows, let our spirits rise,
Finding humor in darkness, our clever disguise.

Embracing the Glow

With soft glimmers bringing smiles near,
We tickle the night into fits of cheer.
A glow stick party beneath the stars,
Makes us feel like we're dazzling czars.

Juggling light like it's a grand feat,
While tripping over our own two feet.
In every flicker, a hilarious jest,
We laugh till we ache; oh, that's the best!

Under twinkling bulbs with our hearts aglow,
We spin around with a whoop and a throw.
With giggles and grins, we loudly declare,
Life's fun without caution, without a care.

So here with the glow, let's cherish the night,
Where humor and joy reflect pure delight.
With arms open wide and laughter in tow,
We embrace every moment, together we grow.

Embrace of the Everbright

In the warmth of the night, we find our way,
With a glow that guides, come join the play.
Tickling the darkness like a friendly ghost,
We dance with shadows, just having the most.

A light bulb flickers, our dance floor ignites,
With laughter that lifts us to dazzling heights.
Glowing jokes fly like balloons in the sky,
As we tumble and giggle, oh my, oh my!

In the embrace of beams that never fade,
We celebrate blunders and never feel made.
Each chuckle a spark, each chortle a glow,
In friendship's warm light, all silliness flows.

So let's twinkle like stars in this fun little show,
With laughter our canvas, and joy on the go.
In every bright moment, we'll cherish our fight,
For happiness dances in the embrace of the light.

Dance of the Radiant

In the glow of a disco ball,
We twirl like we're in a brawl.
With lights that shimmer, spin, and sway,
We laugh our cares all far away.

A leaping beam, it makes us twirl,
Around we go, in a dizzy whirl.
Tripping over our silly feet,
As laughter rings, oh, what a feat!

Each flicker brings a giggling sound,
As we jump up, then tumble down.
Glow sticks waving, we're quite the sight,
In this dance, joy feels so light!

So here we are, a radiant crew,
With shimmery shoes, we'll dance anew!
Forever spinning in bright delight,
In this merry, whimsical light!

Echoes of Dawn

The morning sun, it starts to peek,
While sleepyheads still loudly squeak.
With toast and jam, what a delight,
We tackle breakfast with all our might!

The roosters sing, but oh, so late,
As coffee brews, we'll wait and wait.
Pajamas on, we dance around,
Like moonlit shadows that astound.

We spill the juice, it's quite the scene,
As giggles burst where crumbs have been.
The echoes of our morning fun,
Chasing rays as we greet the sun!

And as the light begins to blaze,
We reminisce in laughter's haze.
For each new dawn is a funny start,
A dance of joy that warms the heart!

Flickering Dreams

In the realm of sleepy beams,
We chase our wild and wacky dreams.
A unicorn with silly socks,
In lands of candy, oh, what a shock!

The moonlit owls wear shades at night,
Hooting jokes that bring delight.
While clouds play hide and seek with stars,
We create the goofiest avatars!

With twinkling eyes, our wishes soar,
In the land of dreams, we laugh galore.
A rollercoaster made of cheese,
We ride with glee, feeling the breeze!

So let the night bring fun and cheer,
As dreams take flight, we've nothing to fear.
In flickering tales, we boldly tread,
Chasing giggles as we go to bed!

Luminescent Paths

On paths of glow, we prance and race,
With silly grins upon each face.
The stars align, and fireflies cheer,
As we march boldly, void of fear!

Each step we take lights up the air,
In a dance of joy, hearts laid bare.
The sidewalk sparkles, oh what fun,
We'll shine like moons, till day is done!

With every giggle, the night ignites,
As shadows shimmer in playful sights.
We leap and bound, like kids at play,
Dancing with shadows that join the fray!

So join us now, in laughter's glow,
For luminescent paths do show,
That humor lights the darkest way,
Bringing joy to every day!

Threads of Clarity

In tangled webs, the laughter spins,
A cat in socks, chasing its sins.
With every twist, the giggles grow,
A dance of joy, a radiant show.

Bright thoughts flutter, like butterflies,
Chasing each other, in silly disguise.
In this silly space, confusion flies,
As clarity leads with winking eyes.

The Silent Glow

A fridge hums softly, a secret joke,
As leftovers whisper, 'We're still woke!'
In shadows, the toast pops up with glee,
While the coffee spills some wisdom, free.

An unseen spark lights up the room,
As the broom and dustpan join in the boom.
They dance together, beneath the bed,
In a silent show, where no one's fed.

Awakening to Brilliance

The sun wakes up with a silly grin,
Wavering beams tease the night within.
With a wink and a nudge, the stars retire,
As dreams giggle softly, caught in desire.

Morning coffee plays a lighthearted tune,
While socks mis-match in a lighthearted swoon.
A cereal box strikes a pose with flair,
In the spotlight of morning, without a care.

In the Embrace of Dawn

The rooster crowed, startled the cat,
Who leaped like a rabbit, 'Now, what was that?'
With a halo of feathers, the morning sings,
As the sun blooms brightly, sharing its wings.

The pancakes flip with rhythm and cheer,
While syrup giggles, 'I'm always near!'
In the embrace of dawn's bright embrace,
Laughter erupts, filling the space.

The Heart of Brilliance

A bulb once sought a friend,
But found itself too bright,
It flickered in the daylight,
And danced with sheer delight.

A star fell from the sky,
With dreams of making cheese,
It landed on a donut,
And swayed in morning breeze.

A candle's whispered wish,
To be a lightbulb one day,
But melted in the sun,
And giggled all the way.

In shadows, jokes were spun,
A glowworm on a spree,
He told the moon a pun,
And lit up joyfully.

Celestial Reflections

The sun wore shades of gold,
As moonbeams played guitar,
They strummed on clouds so bold,
While comets danced afar.

A star tried to impress,
With glittering finesse,
But tripped on cosmic dust,
And laughed, 'I must confess!'

The planets had a race,
To see who'd shine the best,
But Saturn's rings fell off,
And left him quite distressed.

In space, the laughter swirled,
Like bubbles made of light,
In celestial wonder,
They joked throughout the night.

A Beacon in the Mist

A lighthouse had a laugh,
With fog as company,
It winked at passing ships,
And called them all to tea.

A pirate brought a parrot,
Who squawked ridiculous lines,
While waves just rolled with laughter,
In harmony with pines.

The sea, it giggled close,
With ripples full of jest,
While boats exchanged their quirks,
In a buoyant, merry quest.

The beacon blinked its eyes,
And grinned with all its might,
In misty hues of joy,
It shone throughout the night.

Glows of Serenity

A firefly took a stroll,
Wearing tiny sneakers tight,
It tripped over its glow,
And giggled with delight.

A lantern swayed with cheer,
In the garden of the night,
It told the flowers jokes,
While petals bloomed in light.

A moth joined in the fun,
Sporting wings of mismatched tones,
It flapped around for laughs,
With hummingbirds and drones.

In twinkling, soft embrace,
The night was young and free,
With glows of pure serenity,
And sprightly reverie.

Resilient Reflections

In a puddle a mirror, oh so bright,
I see my reflection, what a sight!
With a grin like a cat, and a nose like a pig,
I declare, I'm the king of this gig!

Bouncing back with a wiggle and jig,
Life's a dance floor, silly and big.
I trip on my thoughts, they tumble and spin,
But laughter's the tune, let the fun begin!

In a world made of chuckles, I take my stand,
Chasing after shadows, not quite as planned.
With every misstep, a story is spun,
And I find that the folly is half of the fun!

So here's to the blunders that brighten our days,
Like spaghetti on walls or a cat in a daze.
With a wink and a smile, I rise to the test,
In this riot of moments, I feel truly blessed.

The Pulse of Brilliance

My toast popped up, it danced in delight,
Like a jester in morning, what a sight!
It winks at the butter, it's all in a whirl,
Breakfast is magic, give joy a twirl!

Like a yo-yo of thoughts, my mind takes a dive,
In the circus of caffeine, I buzz, come alive.
Every sip's an encore, a laugh from my cup,
Where the grumpy rejoice, and the sleepy wake up!

My thoughts skedaddle at a whimsie pace,
Play hide and seek in this quirky space.
With a wink and a nod, I chase after dreams,
In a whirl of hilarity, nothing's as it seems!

Amongst the confetti of everyday nonsense,
I'll dance through the chaos without any pretense.
In a place full of giggles, I find my true skill,
For life's just a riddle, and laughter's the thrill!

Flare of Existence

A firefly's a lantern, buzzing around,
With glow-in-the-dark humor, it seldom gets drowned.
It flickers like wishes, in the dark they sway,
A tiny comedian lighting the way!

With a flick and a blink, it twirls through the air,
Making the shadows dance just to dare.
In this chaotic ballet of whimsy and glee,
I find my footing, just me and the bee!

The sun takes a nap, while the moon tells a joke,
The stars join in laughter, no need to provoke.
In this cosmic giggle, we twirl and we spin,
Here's to the joy that's bursting within!

As I chase after stardust and dreams made of cheese,
I tumble through giggles with the greatest of ease.
In this flare of existence, let laughter prevail,
For life's greatest treasure is to relish the trail!

Stars Beneath Our Feet

With shoes made of marshmallows, I bounce down the street,
Each step is a giggle, each leap's quite a feat!
A candy-colored dream, where the giggles collide,
Stars twinkle in puddles where secrets abide.

I trip on my shoelaces, tie them in knots,
Like life's playful antics, it ties up our thoughts.
With laughter as currency, I leap and I bound,
In this magical realm where silliness is found!

The sidewalk's a canvas, my feet splash and play,
Painting joy with each step, in a whimsical way.
Where giggles take flight, and the giggles take lead,
I dance with the stars, oh how sweetly they tread!

And so I find bliss in the absurdity near,
Like a fox with a top hat, I thrive on good cheer.
For life's silly moments feel like poetry's heat,
With stars beneath my feet, oh, what a treat!

Dancing Flames of the Soul

In the kitchen, pots do jig,
Dancing flames, they jump and twirl.
Spaghettis swirl, just like a pig,
Sizzle wins as noodles unfurl.

The toaster giggles, bread takes flight,
Jellybeans bounce, they tap a beat.
A waltz of crumbs, oh what a sight,
Laughing spoons, they can't be beat.

Ovens pull tricks, cookies do sway,
Marshmallows pop like popcorn fun.
A salad toss, just won't obey,
Under the sun, they dance and run.

In this kitchen, joy's uncontained,
Chef hat's bobbing, a comical show.
Spatula's doing a jig, unchained,
In the heat, our humor will grow.

The Wellspring of Brilliance

A fountain of giggles, bright and bold,
Spraying wisdom like confetti rain.
Jokes bubble up, laughter behold,
Genius at play, free from the mundane.

Clever ideas leap from the spout,
They slip and slide, oh what a chase!
Wisdom's a comical scout,
Playing hopscotch in a funny space.

Dancing pencils on the desk do sway,
Sketching dreams with a silly grin.
Each doodle seems to jump and play,
Bursting with laughter from within.

In this well, mirth is the key,
Unlocking doors to clever delight.
Sip on the jokes, come have a spree,
For brilliance shines, oh what a sight!

Horizons of Everlasting Glow

At sunset, shadows prance and leap,
Twilight giggles with a playful wink.
Clouds wearing pink, teasing the sheep,
Stars begin teasing with a blink.

The moon trips over, bright as can be,
Stumbling through beams of shimmering light.
A comedy show for all to see,
Giggles arise in the heart of night.

In this glow, jokes float on air,
Puns take off like kites in a breeze.
Laughter sneaks in without a care,
Joy dancing freely among the trees.

Horizons painted in funny hues,
Chasing the sun till it waves goodnight.
With laughter as our vibrant muse,
We welcome the stars, oh what a sight!

Secrets of the Glorious Dawn

Morning breaks, a ticklish tease,
Sunbeams engage in a playful race.
Roosters crow with such silly ease,
Pillows yawn, still holding their place.

Coffee spills like a giggling stream,
Whisking up dreams that make us smile.
Butterflies burst from a sleepy dream,
Chasing the dawn, oh, what a style!

In this sunrise, jokes take their flight,
Cupboards rattle with laughter galore.
A dance of flavors, oh what a sight,
Morning's mishaps, we can't ignore.

Secrets lie in the golden glow,
Of breakfast fun, a delightful find.
With every sip, our spirits grow,
For each dawn brings laughter, unconfined!

Illuminated Corners

In the corner of my kitchen, too bright,
Lies a jar of pickles, a true culinary fright.
Its glow is a beacon, though they make me grimace,
I dare not eat them, lest I lose my grace.

The bulb flickers madly, a disco in place,
I dance with the shadows, it's quite the embrace.
Spaghetti noodles go flying, much to my surprise,
A gourmet explosion beneath fluorescent skies.

My cat looks like sunshine, with fur so divine,
He's plotting his next move, like he's on the line.
I swear he's conspiring, crafting a plan,
To steal all my snacks, oh that sneaky little man!

So here in this chaos, I laugh and I grin,
In the corners of my kitchen, the fun never thins.
With every big blunder, my worries subside,
In the light of my laughter, my kitchen my guide.

Shadows Dance at Dawn

As the sun peeks up, the shadows extend,
My coffee mug winks, it's becoming a trend.
The toaster is popping, what a sight to behold,
Like an opera singer, it's starting to scold.

I tiptoe around, trying not to wake,
The monster named Monday, for goodness' sake.
With slippers like boats, I sail down the hall,
This morning's a circus, I might take a fall!

The dog's chasing dust bunnies, oh what a thrill,
While the cat's judging me, it's a silent skill.
As birds tweet a tune, I mimic right back,
Could I make a hit song in my pajama stack?

Each ray brings a chuckle, the dark runs away,
The shadows now shimmy, it's a comedic ballet.
In the light of the dawn, we all find our cheer,
Even the grumpiest mug is starting to cheer!

Radiance Amidst the Gloom

In the depths of my closet, a sock has gone rogue,
It flashes bright colors like it's in a vogue.
With stripes and with dots, it revs up the gloom,
Who knew that a sock could disco in my room?

Dust bunnies are gathering, throwing a bash,
They dance on my furniture, oh what a clash!
With each little twirl, they tumble and roll,
While I shake my head, they've taken a toll.

The fridge hums a tune, serenades late-night snacks,
A symphony of leftovers, no need for a sax.
The milk's gone sour, it gives a cheeky smile,
It's a party in here, come join for a while!

Though shadows might linger, and the night may roam,
My world's quite hilarious when chaos feels home.
So let's raise a toast to the quirks and the gleam,
In the glow of the silly, we'll plot the next scheme!

Echoes of a Sunlit Dream

In a land full of pillows, I float like a queen,
Where dreams turn to giggles, and nothing's serene.
With mop monsters lurking, I wield my bright broom,
To chase off the dust while I dance in my room.

My teddy's a sidekick, he's got quite the stance,
He sways to my music, in a fluffy romance.
While the clock mocks my efforts, its tick-tock a tease,
I'll whirl and I'll twirl with untamed expertise.

Each beam that intrudes makes my worries retreat,
I trip over slippers, but oh, isn't it sweet?
With laughter as fabric, I stitch up a day,
In the echoes of cheer, I'm just here to play.

So here's to the dreams, with giggles and quirks,
Where the sunbeams will shimmer, and comedy lurks.
Let's ride on the laughter, like a whimsical stream,
In this world of enchantment, we'll all find our theme.

The Heartbeat of Daylight

In the morning, sun pulls a prank,
Chasing shadows, giving winks,
Clouds giggle as they drift away,
Tickling trees with whispers and chinks.

Roosters wear their loudest suits,
Crowing like they own the place,
While bees buzz with ridiculous moves,
Dancing 'round in a busy race.

The kettle sings a steamy tune,
Reminding mugs it's time to cheer,
Coffee spills with a clumsy splash,
Singing songs the whole world can hear.

Daytime pranks have just begun,
With sunlight sliding on your nose,
Laughter blooms like flowers bright,
In every corner, joy just grows.

Glow in the Distance

From afar, a glowing spark,
Looks like a giant, friendly cat,
Moonbeams tiptoe on the grass,
Chasing fireflies, just imagine that!

Stars are winking, blinking once,
In a sky they've often crammed,
They play hide and seek all night,
Lighting up the dreams we've planned.

A lantern slips and does a jig,
Tripping over all its wires,
A candle laughs without a wick,
As shadow puppets set the fires.

Even the crickets crack a smile,
Singing songs, they love the breeze,
In this silly dance of night,
Glow in the distance, with such ease.

Embrace of the Infinite

In the universe, a sneeze so grand,
Galaxies scatter like confetti flies,
Asteroids stumble, twirling around,
As planets giggle in cosmic ties.

Stars slip on their shiny shoes,
Dancing in a loop-de-loop,
Comets burst with laughter bright,
Creating a galactic whoop-de-whoop.

Nebulas blend in crazy hues,
Like candy spun in a cosmic twist,
With every swirl, they write a tale,
Of a universe that can't be missed.

So hold your dreams with cosmic cheer,
In this vast, eternal show,
The embrace of the infinite, dear,
Brings laughter as we twirl and glow.

Paths Strewn with Gold

On golden roads where giggles gleam,
Laughter echoes with every step,
Each pebble whispers a funny dream,
Inviting all just to interject.

Trees wear crowns of dandelion,
Blowing wishes to and fro,
Squirrels scamper with a sly grin,
Gathering treasures from below.

The sun throws confetti in the air,
While birds attempt a silly dance,
Crickets cracking jokes so rare,
Each path calls for a joyful prance.

So stroll along, take time to smile,
For these paths are never old,
Every stride can last a while,
On trails that are strewn with gold.

Morning's First Kiss

The rooster crows, my alarm clock fights,
Pajamas dance in morning's light,
Socks mismatched, a comical sight,
Coffee brews like a rocket delight.

Sunshine spills like sweet jam spread,
Chasing shadows from the bed,
A wiggle, a giggle, joy instead,
Breakfast toast lands butter-side ahead.

Birds chirp tunes, a merry choir,
Chickens flap, they seem to inspire,
I trip over my cat, oh what a liar,
Claiming victory in this morning fire.

With daylight's wink, I greet the day,
Spontaneous laughter leads the way,
Grab a donut, don't delay,
Morning's kiss, come what may!

The Light's Tender Embrace

Bubbles dance in the sunlight's cheer,
As I scrub my dog, oh dear, oh dear,
He shakes, I'm drenched, never fear,
Joyful chaos, and a puppy leer.

The sunbeams tickle the garden blooms,
While I chase socks in endless rooms,
Laughter dances, excuse the glooms,
This silly life, it joyfully looms.

Rainbows flash from the water hose,
While sprinkles dance on my neighbor's rose,
In this circus, hilarity grows,
Each day, a party, life overflows.

With every giggle, the world's aglow,
A sunny twist in the ebb and flow,
Join the fun, just take it slow,
In the warmth where silly spirits grow!

Silent Brilliance

The moon hides behind a cloud of fluff,
Stars twinkle softly, but that's not enough,
Whispers of night, all cozy and tough,
But the cat thinks he's brilliant, and that's just rough.

While I ponder the vastness above,
My snacks call me, like a gentle shove,
Tumbleweeds of dreams, oh yes, my love,
Chasing the surreal like a playful dove.

A squirrel sneaks by, with plans so grand,
Stealing my fruit, isn't it quite unplanned?
Night's calm giggles, a quirky band,
Even the shadows have trip wires on hand.

Yet, in this silence, there's laughter loud,
With mishaps blooming, I'm not too proud,
The brilliance shines, oh so unbowed,
In the dark, we smile, amidst the crowd!

Chasing the Gleam

A yellow duck flaps in the pond,
Waddling around, oh so fond,
I chase the shimmer and respond,
To laughter echoing on the lawn.

The sun dips low, a glorious flare,
Glimmers dance in the evening air,
Juggling shadows with quite a flair,
As the neighborhood cat gives me a stare.

Frogs leap high with a ribbit cheer,
Their moonlit antics bring us near,
Wings of mischief, that's the sphere,
Under the moon, we shed a tear.

In the chase for shiny, we spark delight,
With giggles mingled into the night,
Finding joy in the simplest sight,
Chasing the gleam, oh what a flight!

Glowing Threads of Existence

In socks mismatched, I prance with glee,
A disco party, just for me.
Lights flicker like fireflies sing,
Oh, the joy that odd socks bring!

A cat in a crown, a dog on a sail,
Chasing cheese it must inhale.
Laughter echoes through the floor,
As silliness dances at the door.

Peanut butter on my face,
A breakfast blend, a gooey grace.
Waffles winking on a plate,
Mornings filled with such a fate!

The world spins in a curious way,
With giggles spilling, come what may.
In every joke, there's warmth to find,
Eccentric joy, unconfined.

Embers of a Brave New Day

A pancake flips and lands with flair,
On my head, it's too debonair.
Syrup rivers flow like dreams,
On breakfast plates, reality screams!

A rooster crowing, quite a show,
He's auditioning for daytime, don't you know?
With feathers ruffled, he struts around,
Such bravery in silliness found!

Dancing to the tunes of morning light,
While cats conspire to take a bite.
Every shadow hides a game,
In this circus, life's never the same.

So let's lace up our shoes, my friend,
And skip through chaos, on fun we depend.
With giggles, we'll pave our way ahead,
In this brave new day, let laughter spread!

Spaces of Rejuvenating Light

In a tea cup town, where whimsy grows,
Flowers wear hats, everyone knows.
Sunshine drips like melted cheese,
Making everyone chuckle with ease.

Rainbows dance on the tips of shoes,
With every puddle, we can't lose.
A laugh escapes the timid rain,
As umbrellas blossom, a joyous gain!

Chickens in shades parade the street,
In a world where oddities meet.
Each moment's a spark, so unrefined,
In spaces where silliness is kind.

Here's to giggles, a bubbly delight,
Where the frivolous dreams take flight.
In every corner, laughter ignites,
In these rejuvenating, funny sights!

Kindling the Twilight Muse

In the twilight where glow worms laugh,
An owl writes poems on a calf.
Stars toss confetti in the breeze,
Oh, how they tease with cosmic keys!

A hedgehog with spectacles, quite the feat,
Recites sonnets to his favorite treat.
With giggles melting into the dusk,
Creativity bubbles, a lively musk!

Moonbeams twirl in a silly dance,
While crickets take their chance to prance.
A party of shadows, weaving their tale,
In this quirky night, we cannot fail.

So let's bask in this whimsical muse,
Where funny sparks ignite and fuse.
In every cackle, the twilight glows,
Kindling the dreams that laughter sows!

A tapestry of Hope

In a room full of socks, mismatched and bright,
A cat wears my hat; oh, what a sight!
Laughter erupts with each little mess,
Hope weaves its magic in chaos, I guess.

The coffee spills over, a slapstick splash,
As dreams tumble out in a fanciful crash.
A quilt made of giggles, we hide from the gloom,
In this fabric of fumbles, we dance and we zoom.

The dog steals my lunch; I can't help but grin,
In tragedy's wake, happiness wins.
So we patch up our hearts with love and some cheer,
In this silly old tapestry, hope's ever near.

The Luminous Veil

Glowing like a toaster, my mom's prized device,
It hums like a dream, serves breakfast with spice.
But when I peek in, what a puzzling sight,
A sandwich, a blender, all stuck, it's a fright!

We drape ourselves in curtains of glee,
Twinkles of laughter waltz in for tea.
Pants on my head, oh what a charade,
In this veil of bright moments, we gleefully wade.

A lollipop sun spills over the floor,
Dancing with shadows that slide 'round the door.
With each cheesy pun wrapped up in a smile,
We find joy in the crackle of life's funny style.

Beacon of Radiance

A squirrel steals my sandwich; what a brave feat,
He cackles in triumph, oh, what a treat!
The sun wraps around us, a warm golden quilt,
We giggle together, no worries, no guilt.

At dusk, the fireflies put on a show,
Winking and blinking, goofballs in tow.
But my shoes are all sticky, I trip on my lace,
In this beacon of giggles, I fall on my face!

Yet laughter erupts like the dawn breaking free,
As I dust off the crumbs and say, "Look at me!"
With each silly blunder, we shine ever bright,
In the glow of our chuckles, everything feels right.

Memories Wrapped in Glow

Wrapped in a blanket that's two sizes too small,
We pile up our dreams, a fantastical hall.
The laughter of ages, a soft glowing sound,
In this cozy cocoon, we joyfully drown.

With glittering thoughts and a sprinkle of fun,
The night wears a grin as we count every pun.
Stories weave around us, like stars in the pitch,
As we share all our secrets, not one silly hitch.

The glow of our memories twinkle like lights,
As we laugh at the past on those whimsical nights.
With love as our lantern and joy as the flow,
We capture each moment, wrapped in the glow.

Paths of Warmth

In a world where winter lingers,
I wear my socks, two at a time.
The sun brings smiles, it tickles fingers,
While my cat plots a heist, oh so prime.

With every beam, the laughter swirls,
My coffee's strong, a daring blend.
The neighbor's dog starts chasing squirrels,
While I just sit, my worries mend.

A garden gnome with big, round cheeks,
Sips lemonade beneath the sun.
While ants parade with tiny peaks,
I grin and cheer, they sure are fun.

So here's to warmth, both strange and bright,
With quirks that dance and tickle the mind.
For in the glow of silly delight,
We find a way to be unconfined.

The Glow of Truth

In the kitchen, pots are dancing,
Vegetables twirl in a merry race.
I'm cooking up a truth, entrancing,
But end up with flour all over my face.

The mirror chuckles, it's a funny sight,
As I concoct my dinner scheme.
A lopsided pie, a culinary fright,
Yet somehow, it tastes like a dream.

The cat steals a bite, with eyes so wide,
While my dog looks ready to plot.
In the glow of my kitchen, where messes abide,
We share laughs over what I forgot.

So in every spill and every jest,
A little truth can shine so bright.
Here's to the cooking, a brave quest,
Where laughter makes everything right.

Light Beneath the Veil

A secret wink from a friendly star,
Hides behind clouds in a playful game.
The moon giggles, not too far,
In shadows where silly jokes reclaim.

With jokes spun tight like a spider's web,
I share a chuckle with the night.
Twinkling laughter from a sleepy ebb,
Turns my worries into sheer delight.

A raccoon in a mask starts to dance,
Finding treasures in the trash he seeks.
In the moonlight, he takes a chance,
This silly bandit sings out peaks.

So here's to the night, mysterious and grand,
With laughter that echoes and tickles the soul.
Beneath the veil, in shadows we stand,
Finding the light that makes us whole.

Shadows that Shine

In corners where the light's not so keen,
Shadows giggle, waving goodnight.
They play hide and seek, oh what a scene,
Tickling dust as they take flight.

A dance of quirks, they stretch and sway,
To tunes only they can hear.
While moonlit scenes come out to play,
They whisper secrets, full of cheer.

Chasing critters who dare to hide,
Each flicker dances with glee.
Those shadows, oh, they take such pride,
In creating chaos, wild and free.

So let us laugh with each little shade,
For in their mischief, joy we find.
In this world of shadows and fun, we wade,
Shining brightly, with hearts unconfined.

www.ingramcontent.com/pod-product-compliance
Lightning Source LLC
Chambersburg PA
CBHW070313120526
44590CB00017B/2657